This Room
in the
Sunlight

Collected Poems

Other Poetry by Bernard Kops

Poems and Songs (Scorpion Press) 1958

An Anemone for Antigone (Scorpion Press) 1959

Erica I Want To Read You Something (Scorpion Press) 1967

For the Record (Secker and Warburg) 1971

Barricades in West Hampstead (Hearing Eye) 1988

Grandchildren and Other Poems (Hearing Eye) 2000

Where Do People Go (The Happy Dragons Press) 2004

Bernard Kops

This Room in the Sunlight

Collected Poems

DAVID PAUL

First published in Great Britain in 2010
By David Paul
25 Methuen Park
London N10 2JR

www.davidpaulbooks.com

Acknowledgements

With thanks to Secker and Warburg, Hearing Eye and The Happy
Dragons Press for the inclusion of poems from earlier collections,
and to Markings who commissioned and published the poem
Anne Frank's Fragments From Nowhere.

Cover photograph: Jonathan Fisher

Printed in Great Britain

For Erica

Contents

Whitechapel Library, Aldgate East

How often I went in for warmth and a doze;
the newspaper room whilst my world outside froze.
And I took out my sardine sandwich feast.
Whitechapel Library, Aldgate East!
And the tramps and the madman and the chattering
crone.
The smell of their farts could turn you to stone,
but anywhere, anywhere was better than home.

The joy to escape from family and war.
But how can you have dreams?
You'll end up on the floor.
Be like your brothers, what else is life for?

You're lost and you're drifting, settle down, get a job,
meet a nice Jewish girl, work hard, earn a few bob.
Get married, have kids; a nice home on the never,
and save for the future and days of rough weather.

Come back down to earth. There is nothing more.
I listened and nodded, like I knew the score,
and early next morning I crept out the door.

Outside it was pouring!
I was leaving forever.

I was finally, irrevocably done with this scene.
The trap of my world in Stepney Green,
with nowhere to go and nothing to dream.

A loner in love with words, but so lost,
I wandered the streets, not counting the cost.

I emerged out of childhood with nowhere to hide,
when a door called my name and pulled me inside.

And being so hungry I fell on the feast.
Whitechapel Library, Aldgate East!

And my brain explodes when I suddenly find
an orchard within for the heart and the mind.
The past was a mirage I'd left far behind.

And I am a locust and I'm at a feast.
Whitechapel Library, Aldgate East!

And Rosenberg also came to get out of the cold;
to write poems of fire, but he never grew old.
And here I met Chekov, Tolstoy, Meyerhold.
I entered their worlds, their dark visions of gold.

The Reference Library where my thoughts were to rage!
I ate book after book, page after page.
I scoffed poetry for breakfast and novels for tea.
And plays for my supper. No more poverty.

Welcome young poet, in here you are free
to follow your star to where you should be.
That door of the library was the door into me.

And Lorca and Shelley said "Come to the feast!"
Whitechapel Library, Aldgate East!

Passover '38

One thing I remember
even more than the hunger.
Scrubbing my knees, smarting my hair and
rushing downstairs
into that playground of my childhood;
where all the other children
with their eyes alight
were building castles with cracker nuts.

I built my castle.
I was a shopkeeper, a millionaire,
I ruled the world;
challenging all to chance
nuts of their own,
gathered from high-pitched aunts
the day before,
as we went from home to home,
running that Yomtov gauntlet
of twisted cheeks and wet kisses.

In those days
families extended forever and ever.

Who wants a castle?
Knock down my castle! I dared.
All in their sudden beauty
the girls came singing, flirting.
Holiday! Passover!

The Angel of Death? Who is he?
A madman on the radio, far away.

Passover lasted for the rest of the year;
the cracker nuts secure
in the lining of my sleeve.
Belonging – we belonged.

Poverty came later,
when most of us did well
and moved away.

Breakdown

All night I dreamed I lay awake
and now the day goes rushing through.
Borrowed from darkness once again,
I find that I have lost myself.
I leave a small note on the table.
Dear Mum, O can U not C how ill I am?
Goodbye.
I rush out through the wallpaper
and walk along the crowded parchment.
Help! Help! Catch me, I'm falling. Hell!
Childcall, birdflight,
down to the endless seas of the never
ending ending night.
The sediment of dusk falls
into the husk of the night.
A spider sleeps and dreams of silver.
Oh, we are the fragments of a dream,
a dream that has no dreamer.

My Brothers

Upstairs they come,
they come for me,
my brothers in their borrowed suits.
They knock staccato on the door
and kick it down with shiny boots.
My friends! My brothers!
They come for me.

An Anemone For Antigone

Written in Belmont Psychiatric Hospital. 1951

Hello my love, Antigone,
all that holds me to the past is an anemone that I hold,
epitome of memory; traded with the Phoenicians
for the last fragments of my sanity.
Swapped my silver shroud for the golden sands
of glass reflections of time and immortality.
Dipped the petals in the violets and purples,
when they stopped to bargain with me, on their journey.
Thrusting my hands through crystal splintering
to the clouds,
gasping incoherencies,
grasping the secrets of shellfish, stars.

Others came and saw the crimson flowing river.
Called it blood and started bandaging.
I ate the rose, chewed the rubber road,
and came away from windows.

Walking about me anxiously,
pulling down lobes, pushing in chins
and puffing out cheeks.
They tell me I am to rest.
Half insane, sad, delirious, depressed and tired of pitying
I walk away to where they lead me; down into madness.
And sit opposite Him,
He who watches me, who murmurs into telephones,
speaks softly in undertones to those
who call themselves my relatives,

at the other end of the line, and crying.
In the winter walls sterilised gowned,
o my love they do not understand.
And all the time I am looking at the plateaus in my hand.
The deserts! Forests, pathways underground. The tubes
and roots.
They ask me questions.
Spasms of staccato silences.
Hell, silence is rocking herself convulsively to sleep.
I do not speak the words I say unsaid. HELP!
Concrete machines are coughing neath an epileptic moon.
O soon it is shed my misery, soon.
Will Dr Lotus come into this room?
I turn my back as bricks disintegrate,
as the ears of walls ooze pus.

I do not want to hold steel, play at soldiers,
smell stenches, kill Christ in the trenches,
see the mushroom bloom of the doom bomb.
I want to hold flowers,
mix pastel shades under trees in cool rooms,
talk with Modigliani, breathe poetry,
weave eternity from the strands of discarded hours.
My myopic memories screech,
so I cut the cords of conversation,
while they weep promises of visiting.
My father makes a speech,
and they leave, return to their dead.

Disciples of Viennese gospels,
now loom the mount above me.

"Say anything you like, lie down,
rest your head, say anything that comes
into your head. No matter how absurd,
there is meaning in every word."
I lie up hill and down, down.
I see a pen scratching over empty spaces,
Christ sprawls crucified a cross the walls,
Scheherazade dances over the desert of Caucasus.
Olives on the golden bough,
Antigone! Ann! Anemone, Agony,
Onomatopoeia's wasteland.
Canticles crawl, cast shadows in the dream.
O can U not C how ill I am?
Fires flickering fingers fumbling in my brain,
my soul was sucked into the slipstream at Shoreditch,
the rubber roads went sliding down the drain.
O, I want to die.
Antigone! Did Dr Lotus pull the chain?
I want to cry. I want –
and they see my tears falling.
I am pelted with words and petalled with pills.
So tell me I can close my eyes and sleep.
They cover me over – but
every now and again
a shadow stoops over me,
it swims through my squeezed tears,
and whispers whisper.
They are going to take me away,
lying with my smiling face to the wall,
they do not know already I am gone.
I have left them, I am crying for joy

all through the cutting of taffeta,
pinching the leaves from the fabric stems,
walking passages of aged greenery
where stone age delinquents bash their heads.
I surf-ride down the spiral screw,
until I come to the sunlight beam,
then bathe my nakedness in the song of spring
and laugh at the death of white bleeding winter.
Here I linger far away,
ripping my fingers through a static stream.
Hello my love! Look I enclose an anemone,
symbolising nothing, save memory.
It is the halo of my afterbirth.
I have thrown myself away but send you my love.
But if you suck on the stem you will find
I have left a little sweetness. A kiss by proxy.

Yes, my love, they have taken me far away,
through the eternity of a suburb
to a place they call Surrey.
It is confusing for I thought I still lie in the room,
yet I am being carried far away, horizontal.
The shadow of trees, budding twigs,
the buds sac'd in the travelling winter and
through the ambulance the somnambulist
impotent sun shines through the mist of frosted glass,
scrapes the sides of my exodus.
Agony O Antigone. I'm gone.
Why do you want to die?
Somewhere I heard them squeaking.
Now we will see if she really loves him.

The road is long. So long.
So if you love me, so long.
Why do you keep on writing to me
on envelope? By the way how is Penelope?
Anyway, how long have I been here?
It seems only today I am in that room
or only yesterday.
A part of me still hangs on to their promises,
their systems of word analogy,
associations with Psychiatrist.
Messiah? Complex? Indigo? Ideas? Idego? Ideology?
Heterhomohetoedipus.
Adler, Freud, adder asp, Electra generator.
Pythagoras. The perversion of
Zink and Zinoviev. Mother? Love! Good! – Go to hell.
The mists of Mystic Jung, Jade vase of Ming.
I will come out, you know,
one day they say. One day.

But when we are young we can do many things,
caress the night away, fly on seagulls' wings,
seek the sun.
We can kiss the streets of the city, laugh, mock God.
But one day when we are old
we are more compatible with the decaying
death mask of this pock marked earth.
When we no longer gaze at each other, but around us.

They say I must synchronise eternity to the big clock tick
they swing and hold to my face closely. I will be
examined soon.

They are setting me to walk upon my feet,
it's time for tears and blood tests.
Now to the office of his omnipotence,
Dr Lotus, who is never there
but is expected tomorrow. I may see him then.
If I walk alone they say one day it is the death of me.
So why do you want to come with me?
And I will always walk alone
because if you want to belong to me
you must become a part of me
and I will still walk alone
Antigone.

The handlines of my palms I read,
those which clutch the headlines of progressive papyrus.
About the coming of the Assyrians.
Christ the Anarchist, Caiaphas the Marxist.

I see Icarus has been taking
lessons from our dear dead heroes
and will attempt another journey wingless.
O black jet of shame.
It comes to pass. I see you in my heart-lines,
mixing lotions of eternal potions
drinking anodynes of powdered glass.
Shaking, quaffing, gazing into witch balls.
Here I sit silently upon the grass, calling fauns,
While you pound your thighs against
my impassiveness. Poised against my poisoned passion.
Like I used to call the Siamese cat,
pouting lipsss and fingertipsss,

and you dancing naked contortions on the carpet.
Pirouettes! Covering yourself
with the woven flower coverlets of divan.
O Antigone, gone.
You will sit beside me if you visit each Sunday
and cry at my laughter and laugh at my tears,
and not understand me.
So throw our wedding lines at me,
divorce our thighs 'neath canopy,
go crying weeping into your hands
unless you really want to come with me
and can get used to tears and agony.
O when our lips have parted and then departed
Antigone Anemone,
I will shout along the long drive! So long.
No one tries to humour me here, when I cry
about the tears of Crocus and the death of Procris
and the Greek allotment of Agony.

I couldn't care less about money,
Except smoke now and again.
Walking silently through the shadow villages
discussing pewter and equations
with God, who has no relations to visit him,
who works out existence with a cats cradle,
sends telegrams to Stanley Spencer, curses Munnings.

The poetry circle of the neurasthenic clique
is presided over by a latter day Yeats,
lecturing about Instinctive Syntax.
Antics with the apples of grace

and Paris and analysis.
I awake in the morning, follow through the funnels
of centrifugal forces, riding on the horses of the
Apocalypse,
holding textbooks of anatomy
and novels by J.P. Sartre.

Narcissus sleeps in deep narcosis.

Volcanoes erupt by the willow tree. Tears cry.
But in reality it is quite boring,
nothing really happens, nobody tells
jokes about madhouses and sex.
O yes! The leucotomised clerk out of deep insulin
has fallen in and out of love with me.
Madrigals by counter tenors beneath my blankets
at four in the mourning.
A chorus of applause, curtains call me to a window,
and I look out over the quiet creaking country
and all are sleeping.

The segments of sediment of sleep.
O, the sexless sighs of Narcissus,
pitched in neuter and feather.
Dr Lotus is on his way.
Furthermore give up mourning,
I have recently seen him walking across Water.
Who knows what may happen yet?
A beautiful Armageddon of Atombomblast
or the resurrection of the dead.
It is all the same.

All the time I am not unhappy but very bored.
Splitting my side with laughter
when they leave me with the angels.
O Christ they do not understand.
But I must go now really,
God is expecting me in the corridor,
to tell me what he has planned for the day.
He knows I have connections with the inside world.
So why do you want to come with me?
And if you love me what is love?
And why do you want to die?
But so-long already, I must leave
empty spaces, words unsaid,
a place for your tears to fall, if you love me.
Antigone! O gone, gone is the agony of the past.
Goodbye. I have to build my bricks of memory.
There is a little hope if you love me.
On second thoughts I shall keep the anemone.

The Sad Boys

The sad boys of the afternoon
are wandering through the town,
looking for some lonely girls
to lay their bodies down.

The sad boys sit around and
croon
but never lose their frown;
no one comes and no one goes;
they watch the leaves twist down.

The sad boys of the afternoon
pull petals from the park,
then throw them at the dying sun
and stroll into the dark.

Questions

What does your father do?
What does he do for a living?

He is a decomposer
and his eyes are open
twenty four hours
of every, every day.

What does your mother do?
What does she do for a living?
She is an earthwife.
and she lies beside him
for ever and ever.
And ever.

Skyman

My God I'm dead
the young man said
when he saw his battered head
petalled on the bleeding sand.
Oh Mother, come and meet me now
and take my hand.
His body like a fountain played
along the empty esplanade.
A Coca-Cola sign winked on
and when the moon came he was gone.

For The Record

They came for him in Amsterdam: my grandfather David,
and with minimum force removed him from his home.

He surrendered to the entire German army,
and that was that.

It is of little consequence now;
so many die alone in foreign lands.
But for the record I must say
they gave him a number, helped him
aboard an eastbound train.

It was a little overcrowded,
but then again they had so many to dispatch.

You might call him part of the biggest catch
in history of those who fish for men.

Anyway, to cut a long story short,
he was never seen again.

I cannot put my finger on the exact day he died.
Nor the time, nor the place.

Suffice to say it was by gas and in the east.

I write this merely to record the facts
for my descending strangers.

Furthermore, today is the 21st of December
in the year of our Lord 1968.
And it is getting rather late.
It rained this evening but now the wind has dropped
and the moon is shining.

It is 11.33 p.m. Precisely.

The Fire Next Time

Next time we are all in the boxcar.
All on the fast track running out of control
towards our final destination.

Next time there will be no selection;
no survivors,
we will all be fodder for the great Moloch.

Next time there will be nothing left;
no-one.

Next time we are all in the boxcar.

Serenade

How many lonely Londons have I seen?
Have I lived without you?
How many times has the Thames torn
me to suicide?
How many times have I died without you?
How many terraces have I searched
for a whisper of your name?
How many times did I try, like this,
to reach you?
Stood on rooftop terrified?
Sighed in cellar, drinking myself to sleep?

How many times did I miss you
by a corner's crooked heart?

I have come through an eternity of smoke
to hear you speak my name.
Borrowed from darkness again
I find at last that I have found you.

Oh, are we then a practical joke
uttered by the total dark?
Are we peopled here in vain?

Listen to my psalm of joy.
Let us not stand on ceremony in this cemented hall.

Let us fall to our knees and crash the bed
before we sleep,
clash together like a cymbal
triumphant and singing,
over the ecstatic streets of London.
The sun is a golden topaz held to hell,
and we are hurled into its spun cocoon
that is called loving.

Train Ride

It rained last night but now
sun sweeps across green lawns.
Blackbirds rise out of yielding winter,
smoking earth waits for spring.
The sky with open arms is showing off.

Beside me is a lovely girl
with long dark hair.
The sun strikes the amber
of her dreaming eyes,
where I am trapped like a prehistoric fly.
She smiles.
I must get to know her.
She is my wife.

Shalom Bomb

I want a bomb, my own private bomb, my shalom bomb.
I'll test it in the morning, when my son awakes,
hot and stretching, smelling beautiful from sleep. Boom!
Boom!

Come my son, dance naked in the room.
I'll test it on the landing and wake my neighbours,
the masons and the whores and the students who live
downstairs.

Oh I must have a bomb and I'll throw open windows and
count down as I whizz around the living room
on his bike, with him flying angels on my shoulder;
and my wife dancing in her dressing gown.
I want a happy family bomb, a do-it-yourself bomb.
I'll climb on the roof and ignite it there about noon.
My improved design will gong the world and we'll all eat
lunch.

My pretty little bomb will play a daytime lullaby and
thank you bomb for now my son falls fast asleep.
My love, came close! Close the curtains, my lovely bomb,
my darling bomb. My naughty bomb!
Burst around us, burst between us, burst within us.
Light up the universe. Then linger, linger,
while the drone of the world recedes.
SHALOM BOMB!

I want to explode the breasts of my wife
and wake everyone.
To explode over playgrounds and parks, just as children
come from schools. I want a laughter bomb,
filled with Sherbet Fountains! Licorice Allsorts!
Chocolate Kisses! Candy floss!
Tinsel and streamers, balloons and fireworks, lucky bags,
bubbles, masks and false noses.
I want my bomb to sprinkle the earth with roses.

I want a one-man-band-bomb. My own bomb!
My live long and die happy bomb. My die peacefully of
old age bomb;
in my own bed bomb.
My Om Mane Padme Aum Bomb, My Tiddly Om Pom
Bomb.
My goodnight bomb, my sleeptight bomb,
my see you in the morning bomb.
I want my bomb. My own private bomb. My Shalom
bomb.

Erica I Want to Read You Something

Annihilation is easier when you are lonely.
But a man who is past it,
who knows no hope, who fears.
Who fears there is no reason
is known to me.

That man knows no order, no purpose,
but only knows a casual shape that has become
familiar.
Yet that man does not sing through me.

It all ends in death.
But when you love someone or detach yourself
from your own sadness,
this loss of life is more felt.

When you have a wife in bed,
a wife warm and passionate and beautiful.
When you are in her and she in you
completely.
When your shadows and personalities merge,
what then?

What of the coming loss, one way or another?

Or can the shape of infinite endlessness
bring a sort of tranquil beauty,
that makes you accept and nicely shrug
and sadly, sweetly smile?

Will I smile? Or will she?
Or will universal destruction take us both
together?
Then we will never have to face the lonely end.
Maybe this is why we want to blow ourselves
to kingdom come.

Oh my love, we must pass on some love.

And so we loved within these sheets,
where I sit within this familiar room,
under this universe; writing this.

Now she sleeps, lost in a book.
I will soon call her name, so as not to be
so lonely. And I shall say Erica
I want to read you something.
I shall call her name and this night will pass;
and so will so many,
and this world will pass and so will so many.
ERICA I WANT TO READ YOU SOMETHING.

Wentworth Street Market Song

"Beggars can't be choosers
so pass the word around,
no matter what you do
you'll end up underground."

Silver trout are sleeping
in heaps upon the slab
with mackerel and
lobsters
and lethargic crabs.
The dead are busy
sleeping
eternity away,
they do not go out
shopping
on this fair summer's day.

"Beggars can't be choosers,
the executioner said;
and if you beg for life
you're bound to lose your head."

They do not smell the flowers
that take your breath away,
Mimosa and Rose, Carnation
and Lily.
The dead are busy sleeping
in the eternal dark,

they do not go out shopping
or walk in the park.

"Beggars can't be choosers
so pass the world away,
no matter how you climb
you'll end up in the clay."

They do not buy the warm bread,
the wine and watercress.
Or give a copper coin
to a bronze accordionist.
The dead are busy sleeping
eternity away,
they come not to the market
on this fair summer's day.

"Beggars can't be choosers
no matter what you're worth,
the best of us, the worst of us
will burst within the earth."

From *The Hamlet of Stepney Green*

Exile

It is raining outside,
it is raining.
The wet leaves are rotting into the earth,
into the sockets of my father's song,
into the mouth of my mother's skull
where she smiles for all eternity.

I am clutched by a cold sadness,
by loneliness, by loss.
Where do I belong?
I feel far away.
But far away from where?

It is raining outside;
far away from the wind on the hills
of my dream,
from the pipes and the birds of my song.

My son laughs in a strange language,
a language I understand too well.

Perhaps I should take my life and death
with me,
walk with my wife and my son and two
blankets,
into the rain.

On a Brief Meeting with Auden

Leaning against the bar
as if receiving extreme unction,
his face amazingly crisscrossed
like Clapham Junction.
Pissed out of his mind in total elation,
beautiful boys surrounding him in
absolute adoration.

Warsaw Pilgrimage

Walls tremble through flame.
Child with no name,
hands up in the air.

The ghetto rubs its smokey paws
over Vistula.
Faces follow prayer into nowhere.

The wind has lost its voice tonight;
yet I hear a song
in a language long since dead.

They say they came with a brass band
the day after we died;
and played a Schubert serenade.

Boy with burning eyes
melting into sky!
Girl, clutching down that cloud,

you are my very own
walls crumbling through flame.

Smoke of children with no name.

Somewhere Over Lonely Meadow

Somewhere over lonely meadow
where the wheat waits for the cut,
a silent exodus of swifts
sprinkle into dying sun.

Somewhere over lonely meadow,
bats zigzag across the moon,
the dozing earth pulls down the sky
and opens trees when dead leaves fall.

Somewhere over lonely meadow
blackberries rotting on the bough
remain unreached by fallen child
somewhere under lonely meadow.

Somewhere over lonely meadow
nothing changes all the time.
The chestnut ripens and the apple;
and the barking of a dog.

Hackney! Sunday! Rain!

Hackney! Sunday! Rain! You know the sort of day.

Black empty trees against a desolate sky.
Expressionless people buying sad daffodils
outside the hospital,
people unaccustomed to flowers except for births,
marriages and death.

So many people come into this place
and so many go out, you know how,
and have their first contact with the earth
in God knows how long.

And here my father is going to die.
I walk to his bed where he smiles at me
although he is already dead,
his milk-white eyes taking,
taking their last look at the world.
He moans, over and over again.
Why? Why am I here? I have no pain.

He has nothing new to tell us, we his gathered children.
A nondescript life sliding into oblivion,
a nobody going nowhere, becoming no-one,
like everyone.
Yet death brings his face distinction,
breeding tells and his skull showing through
is as good as anyone's.
Cancer! Whisper it! Do not let him hear.

Have you seen the doctor? Is there any hope?
What did the sister say?
Someone said someone worse than him
lived for another year.
How long? How long?
How long do you think it will take?

I look out of the window.
Who knows, perhaps he can outlast the world.
Haven't you noticed a sudden deterioration
in almost everything?

The body of the world seems to be wasting away,
the face and the heart and the brain seem to decay,
yet we pray and hope or try to hope and pray,
try to remove the growth to live for another day.

Guilty, that I am not; grieving, because I cannot,
I run out into the world,
try to whistle, try not to weep,
and quickly get the tube away.

Monday

How can I find inspiration
along the Finchley Road,
at nine o'clock in the morning?
How can I laugh or cry, be moved,
be fired by ravenous dustcarts,
gobbling up empty boxes
of Kentucky Fried Chicken?

How can I find two words
to rub together?
Here somnambulists float
down into Underground;
programmed for another dreamless week.
And young girl mothers,
most with their moist bloom
rubbed away,
disgorge their dreams at school gates.

Diaspora

I live in West Hampstead
where happy children
of all ages play
in all languages.

No windows are broken here,
no graffiti.
All in all a pleasant place.
But fears creep in,
fears that drip at three
in the morning.

They rap on the door of my dream
and there in the night
the windows of my synagogue
are shattered.

Whatever Happened to Isaac Babel?

Whatever happened to Isaac Babel?
And if it comes to that –
whatever happened to those old men of Hackney
who sat around a wireless, weeping tears of pride
at weather forecasts from Radio Moscow?

Whatever happened to us? The Lovers of Peace?
And to our proud banners?
Whatever happened to our son?
And to that Picasso dove of peace
we brought him back from Budapest?

Whatever happened to that little man
who tried to leap above himself?
He had a fire in his eyes;
a certain beauty in his eyes.
Or maybe that was merely poverty.

Whatever happened to Vladimir Mayakovsky?
Sergei Esenin? And Leon Trotsky?
Between the Instant Quaker and the Colour Supplement
we are apt to find no time to talk of them.

But then, we are apt to find no time to talk.

Now it is day,
and rather late in the day.
Whatever happened to us?

We are the worm contractors.
Lusty youths of fire have become tweeded teachers,
with a swish hi-fi that was bought for cash
and a smashing collection of Protest Songs.

Oh ye dreamers of peace!
Dreamers of a bright red dawn!
Whatever happened to that dream?

The dead are buried and the years
and forests of computers cover us.
We are crushed within the heart.
We are gone like prophet Leon
with ice-picks in our brain.

But there is no red stain.

We leave nothing behind
except volumes and volumes; such beautiful volumes.
Unread but rather splendidly
displayed upon tasteful teak.

Oh ye sitters down for peace!
Only the pigeons protest
these days down Whitehall.
Oh Comrades of Slogan Square!
This is a windy Judas corner.
This is the fraught, frozen-over winter park.

I smile and walk backward.
If you insist I am also part of this.

But through my clenched teeth.
I somehow cannot stop myself chanting.

Whatever happened to Isaac Babel?
Whatever became of me?

I think often of Isaac Babel,
of his unsung death.
And as I walk away from you
I know that I am all full up.
I am all full up with people.
I have no vacancies.
Suicide at forty would be mere exhibitionism.
Besides, I have songs to sing.
Songs for myself;
songs to keep me warm;
songs to feed into mouths.
And I have one mouth in particular to kiss;
and eyes above that mouth from where I draw my songs.
He was a funny little man, Isaac Babel.
And one would have thought him a nonentity,
had they not needed to dispose of him
so thoroughly in the dark.

You have to draw the line somewhere.

Yes, I think often of that little man
"with glasses on his nose and Autumn in his heart".
Isaac Babel! Can you hear me?
I think often of your untelevised death.

Whatever happened to us
returning from Whitehall
our banners smudged with rain,
our slogans running away?
Us waving, shaving, running after
our going youth and euphoria.
Hurtling through these fattening years
of hollow laughter.

And incidentally – who are we and
where are we?

So dreams die.
My dreams.
So can you blame me for building
barricades in West Hampstead?
Nice flat. Garden flat; unnumbered,
somewhere behind the Finchley Road.
With children laughing and children crying
and within me still one thread of longing.
And one wife calm and warm, belonging.

So – where was I?
Oh yes! Whatever happened to –
what was his name?

Never mind, nothing really changes;
except children grow,
and we realise there is nowhere else to go.
There is only us now. Us alone.
And not forgetting that rather funny

little Jewish Cossack fellow
who at the moment slips the mind.
Not to worry, they're bound to know his name
in Better Books.

There is a certain joy in knowing;
but then again a certain peace and quiet in
half-forgetting.

Children

Who are these strangers come within these walls,
who now are fast asleep?
Their hands do not seem to need
to grasp or guard;
but are opened upward, palms towards the stars.
Why are they surrendering
when they have captured us?

Adam

My son, I have brought you into this;
into this world.
And I have never thought but loved.
Yet had I thought I would have done the same,
and I would never have you unborn,
and I have always loved your name,
since I threw my flame into another flame
and held you weeping when you came.

A girl and I and one night loving
dreamed and dredged you from the stars,
and up you came.
I loved your mother and I love her,
and I put you into her,
and now my love walks with you.

So be gentle in the night.

It is customary my son to tell you things;
to show you the way.
I who am lost and burning and trembling in the dark.

These words then are instead of words,
instead of tears.

So there you are; here.
Survivor from the night,
refugee from space. Smoke you are,
taken shape.

Beautiful child in the ghetto of your mind,
lost within the congregation of your shadows.

My son! You have your head, your heart, your soul.
Your name, your fears, your face.
No-one can die your death or live your life.

We see you trying to take your place,
and search the questions that cloud your face,
we hear you singing with the worm,
we watch you struggling to conform.
And though your tears tear us apart
somewhere we are glad.

They can swim my son.
They can negotiate roads and sky and water
and rooms packed with people.
Falling in the garden does not cause them to drown.

Out of the window I see you all alone,
pursued by all of them.
But they do not see that you are pursued
by all the aeroplanes from within.
They do not hear your singing rabbis weeping
centuries of psalm and dust.
They do not smell these fearful faces of the past
who haunt you,
that cause the tears to fall along your lovely head.

Take care. Go through your way and come out
as you shall.
Out of your shell of troubled sleep.

I sing of times when these words have no meaning,
of a girl and you and one night loving;
who dream and dredge me up from dark.
Until then I hail you in your hell.
Become familiar with the stations of the star
so that you may truly enter out of pain.

And try to smile.

Hannah

My daughter lives! She lives.
She will not die tonight.
She will outlive me after all.
She will rise up in all her beauty.
Her eyes, her almond eyes will not be closed
forever.
She has come through and does not die
with this endless night.

When that never-coming telephone call
came,
and the spine of night was cracked
by that sudden bell,
I was polite and thanked the doctor,
said I was pleased she was out of danger.
She has come through, sailed right through
the hungry dark.

Hannah! Your eyes will move again.
And your hands.
And you will sing.
And that is how you prove you are alive
and therefore you will not be thrown away.

And you my friend, you too must get some sleep.

Abigail

This morning
Abigail discovered her shadow
and cried.
Later she ventured
out of the dark,
dancing into the light.
She would have been used to sun,
had the Temple
not been destroyed.

Rebekah

The river. So often the setting of my sorrow,
I wept you.

She came smiling out of the dark,
her laughter lapping against the stones
of my years. Etching joy.

She brings gusts and gales of laughter,
sailing me far from my own dark sea.

My daughter.

Exile 2

How sad that I have found nowhere.
And I cannot dance in these streets.
I have found no dream.
I come from nowhere and go nowhere.
This is a land without dream;
an endless landscape.

How beautiful for those who can reap
their own sunset,
who can grow their own fruit
out of their own sweat.
Beautiful for those in their own land,
whose laughter and tears soak into their own land.
Whose songs fill the earth and the sky
of their own land.

How beautiful to dance and live
and die in a country with a dream.

My tears fall into the brick and haste
and death of day-to-day existence.
This is a country with no dream
and no-one notices that I am crying.
By the waters of my own four falling walls
I wail.
I hear the trumpets, see the invisible
worms of destruction working away
in every corner.
How sad that I have found nowhere.

My children and my grandchildren
have no festival.
This sun no ceremony.
How sad that the seas beyond do not lift me.
Nor the hills.

Yet, far off
in my dream, I still hear the reeds singing,
and the tambour.
And the family; one single thread
that binds me to this fearful
and beautiful mystery called life.

Operation

You'll be alright, Erica said.
But darling, I could end up dead.
Then, going down into the anaesthetic
universe, I give a long drawn out sigh;
you know, the Esperanto of the Jewish World.
In return she gives birth to an incredible smile;
somehow that alone makes life worthwhile.
But as they wheel me away
through the door I cry:
"If you let me die I won't talk to you anymore."

Rosh Hashana

Today we will go to Regent's Park
with our daughters and our son.
We will stand beneath a chestnut tree
and aim as high as clouds for conkers.

Our laughter will rise into the sky
above these clouds, higher than
those other sounds
our children do not seem to hear.

Then, hungry, we shall hurry home
and spread our harvest all
around the floor.
And I suppose we shall sing,
for songs are the dreams
we capture from the dark;
songs and prayers of the irreligious.
Meanwhile all this will have to suffice
for miracles.

Erica By Lethe

You wandered along the shore
considering the other side;
and I watched you, helpless.

There was nothing I could do
as I waited,
with all the nerve endings
of my love exposed;
unable, useless.
For the first time somehow at a loss.

You looked back at me,
your calm eyes floating above your pain,
as if weighing things up,
considering perhaps that I
would give you an even rougher ride
if you returned to us.

But it was for you to decide.

You chatted to the Boatman,
haggled for a while,
then suddenly you decided not to cross.

And so you came back to us, smiling.

Our Kids Have Just Left

We sit here rather dazed;
our kids have just left home.
We gave them all our love,
they raided all our dreams
and ate up all our jam,
and left us just like that;
and laughed all down the road.

Our kids have just left home.
And oh the sweet relief.
Come, let's postpone our grief
and please answer the phone.

They're coming three o'clock!
And staying for the night!
Where did we go right?

Henry Williamson

...eted me, smiling.

...face I couldn't quite place.
His name was on the tip of my brain.
His eyes, a pale cornflower blue
pinioned mine.
A steady, courageous, English stare.

Do I know you? I said.
And such a charming soft smile!
There, on that windy pavement
it suddenly dawned. Of course!
You are Henry Williamson!

"Yes!" He replied. "For my sins!"
Then the darkness dawned.
There I was faced with a writer
of considerable fame.

There is always something suspicious about
authors who write about nature.
Yet he had such a nice, such a handsome face.
Henry Williamson! Ah! *Tarka the Otter*!

"Yes! And you I believe are of the Jewish persuasion."
His charm oozing an aura of sweet doom.
I laughed. And then the rest of his past
dredged up from the deep.

Wasn't there a photograph of you and Hitler
laughing together?
It all came flooding back.
Didn't you dedicate a book to Your Führer?
To the genius across the water?
"Yes! I did! But I tell you this,
had I known what was going on
I would have gone in there myself and
pulled those Jew boys out of the flames."
Smiling, he shook my hand and hurried away.
I could not move. I grinned and froze.

Perhaps I should have punched him on the nose.

Poor Old Crow

Note from a nature article: *"Crow parents almost work themselves to death trying to feed their voracious young."*

I feel so close to crow.
I hover limp and ragged, croaking low.

I who sought the highest tree, so tired now;
I flap so slow. But I'll find the strength
to wave goodbye, for soon they'll go.

They'll leave poor crow,
poor thankful crow.

I'll sigh – oh dear, must you go?
I'll cry.
I'll hide my wicked beady eye,
so full of glee.

I watch them practise flight,
day and night I hear them rise
and fall.

I've seen it all.
How terrible my children,
must you go? Must you leave old crow?

Oh soon I also want to go.
I want to fly away with lady crow,
I want some years of gluttony,
for me.

Hall of Mirrors

He came for me tonight with shooting stars.
He came towards me in the dark
firing crimson grass.
I love you my brother, creeping through the dark;
I wait for you to hurl the flash and chant the black.

He came for me tonight and sang the trees.
Into the hall of mirrors he scattered eyes.
We elongate, distend and try to pray
and point and grimace, laugh; then blend and sway
into the passage of our father's psalm;
and end our dream of days and shattered glass.

Shattered glass always figures in my dreams;
in this hall of mirrors where I wait for him.
I wait for him to roll me up in earth,
to take me to the ocean made of mothers' tears.

On Meeting Allen Ginsberg in Tel Aviv

In those days gallows humour
was the real currency.
It was the usual hand to mouth,
touch and go existence.

The State was having its Barmitzvah
and we had been up to Jerusalem
for the sake of our soul;
and to replenish the hole in my pocket.
But now it was time to go.

Jerusalem, having witnessed
everything, since our world began,
did not weep at our departure.
The eternal lemon walls smiled
and clapped their hands.

And so we went back into the real world.
It was downhill all the way.
Sadly we returned to Tel Aviv,
knowing we had left our hanging hearts behind,
and found Hayarkon Street deserted.

It was Erev Rosh Hashana.
Our crumbling house was on the beach;
and zooming in from the sea
a million buzzing flies greeted us.
And an army of ants devoured our thoughts,
when we entered our derelict flat.

Longing for bed and sleep
we dived straight for the bedroom.
"And maybe a little love before schluff."

"Someone's been sleeping in my bed."
My beloved said, opening the door.
Then the unforgettable head
sprang from beneath the sheets.
And smiled.

Out clambered the poet, Lazarus like.
"Hi! Bernard Kops. I'm Allen Ginsberg and
this is my lover, Peter Orlovsky. And
thank you so much for letting us borrow
your room."

The poet minstrel of New York
tried seducing me with his smile.
"My pleasure." I lied in such a way
to show I was fucking fed up.
"Orlovsky! Wake up." The poet shook the foetal
shape. It stirred.
And the gay goy boy emerged, one quarter awake,
blew a sleepy kiss, then returned to bliss.

Later, over coffee Allen forgave us
for being less than delighted
that he had purloined our space.
"What can you expect of a poet?" I joked.
"Please forgive my chutzpah." He laughed.
And soon we all puffed away to paradise.

"Hey! Kops! These are the high holidays.
I hear there's a small shule somewhere near,
where we can get high on prayer."
And offering more dope, He dived
into his clothes. "Let's go there!
And get good with God."

We refused in a very English sort of way.
"Thank you so very much.
But we would like to rest today."

"Okay! I'm off to visit Martin Buber."
And he was out of the door.

In the evening we walked along the deserted shore.
There was a feeling of the end of the world.
Our infant son pointed joyously
at the golden tightrope of horizon.
We deeply breathed in the angry sea
and the fresh September air.

Allen came back later. "Guess what!
I pulled the old man's beard."
We gasped.
"He was angry. He was outraged.
I left hurriedly.
I thought being a great philosopher
He would understand."
Allen again offered us his joysticks.
We refused. He shrugged.

"Kops! Kopsess! And little Adam Kopskin!
It's been such a lovely day. But we must leave
tonight. This place is beautiful but dead.
We've had a wonderful time. Thanks for
your kindness." He said.
"Yes" I replied. "It was rather nice."
"It was miraculous, meeting Martin Buber.
But now we must be off to Castro's Cuba."
He rhymed and waved and off they went.
He now belonged to the past.
The past of all poets.
Everywhere to go and nowhere to belong.

How sad, how glad we were to see them go.
We hoped they wouldn't miss their flight.
and we had somewhere to sleep that night.

Jessica Three Years Old in Thatcher Days

You sing in your doll's house;
chatting to no-one,
oblivious to us.
Lucky you.
Stay there as long as possible.
There is nothing here
that we can offer,
except greed and chaos.
And sadness.
Your dolls do not queue in the supermarket.
They do not see their fraught reflections
at the Checkout. How angry they have become.
How quietly mad they have gone; how tragic,
how despairing, trundling home with baskets full
of empty lives.
Your dolls do not pass the young old,
sleeping on pavements, unloved,
unloving.
They belong.
They are valued in your universe.

You play in your doll's house,
unaware of the Medusa on the box,
with her head of snakes;
her Ministers;
who hiss their sweet venom, their arrogance,
so that we too fall sick, pass on their contagion.
This is not Rome of the crucifixions.
Not Egypt of the Pharoahs,

Nor Babylon.
Nor the Black Death of the Middle Ages.
This is Britain, 1988.
Granddaughter, these are the Dark Ages.
Yet you remain unaware.
Immune to all this desperation.
Stay in your doll's house.
All your invisible friends have come for tea.
And your laughter falls like golden rain,
reminding us there is more that greed
more than pain.
I pray that by the time you understand these words
the plague would have passed,
and the world and you can emerge out of darkness.

Jessica, Stay Three

Your laughter is a waterfall in a desert of traffic jams.
Don't grow.
Don't grow and go to school.
They will cram your head with garbage,
pluck the joy right out of your eyes.
What will they teach you that you do not know?
That you must love and be loved?
No!
They will shove numbers into your head
They will numb you with the science
of their survival.
They will teach you how to eat your friends
as well as your foes.
They will fix you.
At eight you will be talking of security, mortgages,
pensions.
At nine, endowment policies, shares.
At ten they will teach you how to own the world.
You will be old so soon.
You will forget how to sing;
once they have got their claws into you.
Climb the climbing frame!
Swing upside down.
Cartwheel. Be a disgrace. Cover your face and dress with
such unholy mess. Roll on the grass.
Scream and love yourself.
Dance under the moon.
Flout your nakedness;
astonish every house.

Shout with wonder, joy,
when you suddenly notice stars.
Don't go! Stay where you are.
Stay three.
And run towards me,
holding wide your arms,
laughing like the end of this world.

Success

All my children talk to me.
More or less.
And I have loved the same woman
for fifty-four years.
I suppose you could call that success,
if you ignore the pain
of almost everything.
And what's more we've been together
and stayed sane.
More or less.
Yes!
Despite the encroaching endless mess;
the heartless conversions
that threaten to engulf West Hampstead,
I still maintain my ridiculous oasis.
And here sometimes even neighbours
manage to smile and nod.
And my granddaughter thinks that I am god.
Why am I such a lucky sod?
More or less.

Three in the Morning

Looking at photographs,
there is one face in the darkness.
One recurring image.
Erica throwing flowers backwards
over her shoulder,
high into that black sky.

I think often of nothingness
and the fear, the chill at three in the morning,
of the absurdity of being and not being.

Those Irises!
That purple explosion in that winter of poverty,
when we lived on laughter.

Anya Three Years Old

Holding my hand and deep in sky,
she was too silent,
I asked her why?
She stared up at me
and then replied.
God filled me with blood,
so I'm alive.
I like my blood in but not outside.

Kosher Cannibalism

I love my wife deliciously
and the earth she floats upon.
She is extremely edible,
even with her clothes on.

Chloe

Out of the darkness of nothing
she arrived,
pulling into this harbour,
the shores of West Hampstead.
As if not terrified
of the millions of aeons
that surrounded her journey
to us.
She came by way of Diaspora Umbilica,
taking in the songs and sorrows
of Odessa,
the cries of Riga, Amsterdam,
the sighs of Dublin
the winds of Dartmoor.
And now she manages to sit up
with such delight,
holding out her arms, staking her claim
to all of us with smiles.

Bagel Song

Remembering Ginsberg's "Howl"

I have heard the songs of lost goys, seen
them throw their kosher wives away for
Shiksers; an easy fix to score a dark
oblivion.
I have watched them chase away
their dreams for gay Gurus in shyster
shopping Malls;
and dived into myself at Moma.
The Museum of Modern Fart;
where I found God,
who ripped me off during a fake mantra session
in downtown Manhattan, before a hot Mandala.

But I have come through, oh my brothers!
And now I sing of the universal Bagel.
International panacea. Hot from the oven of
Yahweh, at Louis' Delicatessen on the Lower
East Side, New York.
Open Sesame Seed Bagel!
Or maybe a crammed Get High
Poppy Dream Bagel!
Surrounded by a coleslaw sea and
a salt beef mountain.
Yeah! Yeah! Oh Yid! Here we sat down and
played our harpies by the Waters of Manhattan,
singing "Make Bagels! Oh my friends, not War."
And comrade! You who dreamed of a bright

red dawn. Hurl away your hammer, smash your
angry sickle. Oh Comrade! Come! Join me.
Join me in love.
Take a bite of my sweet and sour pickle.
And as for you! Oh Goy! Enjoy.
Join in our feast of joy.
Tear away your crown of thorns,
and forget your star in the East.
Your bed of nails!
Your holier than thou Christian pie
in the sky.
Bite my blissful blintz, my Pastrami on Rye. And
I shall try to put aside
The Father! The Son! And The Holocaust.

Umbrellas

Where have they gone?
The faces I know
False teeth and glasses
and shoes in cupboards.
Discarding their debts
and loved ones.

How inconsiderate of them.

Where do people go?
The faces I know.
Why do they suddenly vanish
leaving umbrellas behind?

Birth of Isaac

Isaac came to a river.
It was so wide
he couldn't see the other side.

He didn't know where he was
or how he got there.

Then he saw another boy
swimming towards him.

He was beautiful. What's your name?
The swimmer said.
I have no name. I'm only just born. He cried.

Then we shall call you Isaac.
It means laughter.

And so Isaac became Isaac.

What's this river called? Isaac asked.
This river is called life.
My name is Max, the swimmer said.
Now we must get to the other side.
I can't swim Isaac cried. I'm only just born
Isaac laughed.

Jump on my back, Max commanded.
I am your brother. I'll take you across.
And Max laughed and laughed.
And their laughter joined together
and echoed all across the water
as they made for the other shore.

Poems Are Like Grandchildren

Poems are like grandchildren.
You should never bribe or persuade them
to visit you.
They must turn up on their own accord
and when their faces light up your eyes,
you should never rush to embrace them
at the open door.
But wait until they enter and overwhelm
and delight you.
Never ask will you stay?
They may well need to rush away.

Poems are like grandchildren,
they come close in their own good time.

Four in the Morning

Going back to bed at four in the morning
Erica sleeping; smiling as she surfs
the dark waves of all our ocean years.
Enclosed in this embrace I laugh
at all those who will wake believing
today will be different from yesterday.
And at those who believe
that today will be the same as yesterday.

Going back to bed.
The tightrope before dawn. The balancing act.
Vision of grandchildren, negotiating the chasm;
the singing strand trembles.
Sometimes I soar and fall
and find myself bouncing in the air.
Sleep images floating
as I slowly motion my stance
back into the slow safety of cobalt skies.

Grandchildren so easy dance upon the wire.
Jessica, our golden apple.
Daughter of daughter.
You have me reaching
for my heart and my pocket.

And Chloe the newest.
I breathe in the smell of the universe.
She stands before she can crawl;
and laughs when she falls.

And Anya taking her place, inhabiting her space.
How madly human we are. We deserve ourselves.
Oh! The unbelievable beauty of this world.
The music of being, of being Max
the prince who will roam the cosmos
with his sword of stars.
Grandson; your path points in every direction.
Your breath. The sweet wonder of this world.

And Isaac, not yet here. Yet I can hear him
Playing football with my heart.
In fields not yet there.
Living cantatas of spring, emissaries
into the future, proving all this
will exist.
Soon. Forever.
And now I can swim
the cosmos and return to us.

Two Tall Ladies

Sometimes when stalking sleep
I wander the communal garden.
Three a.m. The grass weeps.
No children on the swings.
No sound,
except the curdled silence
of dreams.
Soon I see my long dead
neighbours.
Old men and women
playing slow motion tennis
on courts no longer there.

Two tall ladies are not there tonight.
Both tucked up beyond death.
The two of them went
and years and years pass away.

One day they died.
And did not wake.
Jill with her cat curled into her.
Maggie still holding her husband's
hand.

When I close my eyes
I call them again. And they appear,
oblivious to us,
floating across the grass,
both as high as moon.

Our two tall ladies,
white faces, green fingers
pruning bushes, trees,
tending flowers,
chatting away, as always
with so much to say,
but silently.

Then laughter without sound.

There they go, but I see them still
holding the strings of community
together.

They were the fulcum.
Neighbours gathered.

Jill and Maggie were centre stage.
They gave us cohesion.
In those days our garden went on forever
and ever. Things worked, flourished.

From their gaze flowers sprang.
They fixed things.

But one day they died
and did not wake,
and nothing could bring them back.
And Spring after Spring came
and went.

When the eulogies hurried past,
Jill slipped away and Maggie
entered, and followed her.

Now and forever they both lurk
in the dark green lawn
of my closed eyes.
Maggie watering her flowers,
singing to herself.
And Jill still smiling, waving and
watering her wild pear tree,
springing from her own ashes
that were sprinkled there.

I shall never see them again.
But I shall always see them
in the garden.
Tonight and forever,
bending over their blossoms.

I'm waiting here for day,
for the pears to ripen,
to taste their goodness.

And in the day our garden
loses its memory.
But there they go,
merging into the green,
two tall talking ladies, wandering,
gone back into the dark.
When they died community died.

The Third Age

I remember when I was an old man,
I harangued the clouds.
I was quite irascible and growled
and thwacked passers by
with my walking stick.
And cursed down cul-de-sacs.

When boys kicked a ball too close
I rushed to get there first
and punctured it with my false teeth.

And thus I journeyed
all the way to Lethe,
knowing I was unloved, unloving.

But I did not cross the river
because
there was nothing on the other side.

And so I wandered back towards second
childhood,
laughing and gurgling
at practically everything.

And shouting over the Heath,
"Life is! Life is!"

People now smile at me as I pass.
And that is somehow quite nice.

To a Neighbour

How often I saw you in the garden.
Your breath hovering, turning the grass acidic blue.
Pruning your own progeny,
admonishing the little children tumbling
on the slide.
Promising them
the scaffold if they laughed too loud.

But now, sour angel, you are dead.

Wasps no longer fly from your mouth.
Your lies are buried with you.
I no longer taste
the nausea of your gossip.

The other night
when I heard of your dramatic exit,
I could not believe my luck.
I could hear the children
cheering in their sleep.
And I raised a glass and a smile.

But now I find it hard to bestow a curse
on your grave.
For you have joined the faceless
legions and are wiped clean.
And all my hatred and dreams of revenge
have flown away and followed you.

Distance has somehow made you human.

Cats

They stare from windows with eyes of hate;
in every room they watch and wait;
in every city, so smugly curled.
Cats are waiting to take over the world.

Nightcall

The phone ringing
tears my dream apart.
What? Where am I? I murmur
to the shape beside me.
Who are you?
She comes into focus.
I think she is my wife.
And I cascading into life
shoot the moon back into my body.
"The phone!" She says.

What time is it?
What time? What is time?
Three a.m.?
Time when people die
and get reborn.
I Lazarus over.

This time of night?
Who else has gone?
When the phone rings at three a.m.
It is never to your advantage.

A voice rises from the pit,
from the dark gravel
of the past.

"Bernard! Is that you?"
Who knows who is me?

"Bernie! This is Len."
Len?
"You know! Len!
Bernie! One thing I ask!
I'm going to die,
please write my obit."

I groan a cloud
and wrap myself in silence.
"You are the only one.
The only one I trust."

Someone trusts me?
That *schnorrer*?
Len the writer? Call him a writer?
He barely had two words
To rub together.

His voice hasn't changed.
Those sonorous golden syrup words.
Belonging to lost years in Hopper
cafes.

Len it is. A lost fiend friend with two heads,
I thought he had died years ago.

He regales me with memories I cannot recall.
And pulls me back
into those pre-plastic streets
by the strings of apparent friendship.
"Please Bernie.

You're the only one
who knows me well enough
to do me justice."

His voice now demands. Commands.
"You will do it. You must."
As if I owe him something.

But Len! You are not
the dying sort.
His laugh is a man twirling
on the gallows.
He never lets go.
He implores, laughs. He skewers me with stories
of our exploits.
The times we ran through those
dark night streets shouting
"Take a fucking Rimbaud at the moon!"
Did we do that?
He recalls places, times, events where I was not.
I seem to have no choice.
I agree. I must agree. He goes.
I coalesce back into the night
and sleep the sleep of the unjust.
Surfing the milky way again
into the black hole.

It is ten a.m. when the bell tolls again.
At the other end it is the editor
of dark celebrations,
of births and deaths.

"Leonard is dead.
Will you write his obit? He wanted only you. Will you?
Four hundred words?"
I laugh.
I laugh, growling like the lost
children of Soho.
I am consuming a black river
of coffee as I make with the words.
Holding back the torrent of anger
The bastard. The *gonif*.
I curse as I pour out the honey of words.

"Good friends have the audacity
To desert one." I write. "The world is a
shivering square of loneliness without him.
Leonard was a unique and special being.
He achieved the heights that are seldom scaled.
His greatness he has left behind. He towers
above us all. He is more alive dead
than all of us who survive him.
Leonard shall be sorely missed.
He has gone. He is dead.
He slipped into the universe
with consummate ease, I believe."

It was Lautremont I believe who said.
"When I am dying keep my friends away.
Bring my enemies close.
At least I know where I stand with them."

I am in the garden delirious with joy.
I chirp with the birds.
Suddenly the world is so beautiful.
It is now proper day. In the streets
people are clock-worked into life.
I am happy, so happy in the morning.
Inside I close my eyes and bathe
in the smell of toast burning.
I go back inside to eat slices piled high
with French apricot jam.
I pour some more of the black magic stuff
and dance around the kitchen
with my eyes closed,
slowly, ever so slowly, to the deep sweet sounds
of Gabriel Fauré.

Night Visitor

He came into the room quietly and smiled.
I nodded, smiled in a different way.
He sat down. How are things he said.
Things are marvellous I sighed.
Good, he replied.
Have you met the family?
Many, many times he said.
Good to see everyone so well.
Nice. He offered his hand of ice.
Glad you dropped in. Did you come through the door?
Last time, you slipped through the window?
Why these sudden visits? It's twice this week.
What's it all for?
I whispered, but the others did not seem to hear,
all caught up in the web of their lives.
Their dreams of life.
So. What can I do for you? Cup of tea?
Chocolate biscuit?
Thank you. Laughing he pushed my offering away.
So why? Why? I'm feeling fine. In the pink of life.
Just checking, keeping my eye on things.
And now I must be on my way.
Be seeing you.
Yes, I said.
You're almost a member of the family.
And all words with him were spent.
And off he went. The mirror path.
And all I could do was laugh and laugh.

Did you say something she said, surfacing from her book.
No, just talking to myself.
So what's new?
You are. Every day.
Come to the window. What a sky!
And the scything moon! Look!
But no-one was there except the wind
and the clear, purple sky.
And I laughed and laughed and touched her face.
And another day and another day sailed by.
I love you more than life I said. And more than death.
Let's go to bed.

Life

Every morning I wake
and everything is where it was
yesterday.

The sky! The trees!
The woman who lies beside me.

Music floats through the window.
A phenomenon of birds
sing on bare branches.
And fresh shoots peep
up through the earth,
into the world of my garden.

Then the sky lights
and day and
family appear.

Yes! This is my house.
My heart beats.
I look in the mirror,
I am reassured.
I am here and there is somewhere
in this strange place to walk
and sing.

Love Song For Fifty Years

Erica! Look! Look! The sharks are slowly circling
in the sky. Poet for lunch.
How do you put up with me?
How can I put up with me?
If I were not me I would have left myself years ago.

Walking home from Kenwood, I wander. I wonder.
How many years? Erica, how many years?
Erica! I see your face and wonder who you are.
A face I have floated and juggled these fifty years.
Or is it fifty thousand?
How many times? How many times, again and again,
have I invoked your name?
One hundred and seventy eight
thousand times to be exact.
Erica! The years are scuttling clouds.
Memories, faces, names coalesce.
It's called living.
Is this your face in the mirror of the pavements?
Or mine?
She turns, sings a chrysanthemum
that rings across the mountains and
the meadows of West Hampstead.
As beautiful as the lemon walls of Jerusalem.

Days and nights and years flash by.
My dead aunts sigh in the sky.
The rain slants, cuts the sky.

Erica! Where are you?
She's gone! In a flash! Faces congeal
around her. Ah! There you are. Across the grass,
along the aisles of Waitrose,
hurrying towards the fish counter.
Erica!
Please come back.
You are the only one who can direct me
to where I am.

Love Song for Erica's Breasts

Magnets make certain artefacts
fly to them.
Such are my lover's breasts,
dizzying in a drunken dance,
attracting my hands.
Two urgent babies clutching
those domes of silk
for the beautiful milk of eternity.
Oh how eagerly they drink,
opening the safe,
allowing the jewels of joy
to escape and dazzle
away the darkness of the morning.

Waking Dreams

Somewhere deep in the house
that now isn't there, I hear a young woman
softly crying clouds.

Now all my grandchildren come.
Those born and those not yet arrived.
They play football in the sudden street.
And the great ball of fire sails through the sky.
The laughter! The sobbing mother!
My sisters, my brothers, getting on
with their lives, their dreams. Their daymares.
My unborn ancestors. All are there
surrounding me. I conjure births and exits,
deaths and entrances. I furnish dreams.

An old man shuffles along the road.
It could be me.
I try not to catch up with him.
But he turns and smiles
"Don't grow old." He scythes.
When he drops dead I walk over him.
He could have been my father.
I never etched his face.
I will never grow old.

In the world of waking, the world of true dreams,
where people are plucked so suddenly,
leaving leaves and debts and sky,
and grandchildren who will hug you,
and lovers to weep in a back room, we have no choice.
It is still not such a bad place if you furnish dreams.

The Internet

Erica! This infernal, marvellous Machine.
Everyday,
at several times,
I make love with my fingertips.
I tap in your name. You are my password.
I cannot touch the world
until I touch you.

Happy New Year

The woman in the funny hat smiled when she saw me.
Then she crossed over; her thick Paris perfume arriving
slightly before her.
Little frayed cloth flowers adorned her halo.
She was wearing synagogue black.
At first she was unusually lost for words;
her skin a collapsing pastry crust.
Her eyes drowning in the weeping of her years
cried out for help.
Then she unloaded her burden.
"My lover died in my arms," she sighed.
"Last Thursday. Three a.m."
I commiserated, naturally.
"Every day they raise this road just a few inches higher."
she laughed,
and slowly she continued her puffing journey
to the main road.

Today it was different. The rain never arrived.
The candles in some windows were alight:
singing defiantly into this dark world.
And there she was again, that same woman as always;
over the road, her eyes falling upon me.
But this time she did not cross.
Only her furtive smile accosted me.
And her gaunt face, belonging to the desert,
of a tribe lost long ago.
So alone. So lonely. Staggering through the sands of time,
still sighing at the angry sky.

She should be waving a myrtle branch
Instead she turns and murmurs "Happy New Year."
As if afraid that others might hear.
Now she moves ever so slowly,
as if climbing the impossible hill
of Canfield Gardens towards Waitrose.

Lethe

The boatman smiled
as he gently rowed me across
the dark water.

Do you come here often? I said.
He laughed, deep down in his throat
and winked at me.
A special familiar smell
pervaded him in the moonless night.
The scent of my mother's body.
"Enjoy!" He said
as we reached the other shore.

On Hearing of Adrian's Death

Suddenly across the road
I saw the man, smiling.
He waved at me.
I wavered back.
He nodded. Then cooed.
"By the way, do you know the abode
of the poet, Adrian Mitchell?"
I shook my head, anxious to get away.
Then like a mischievous boy
he pointed to the door of my friend.
"Look! We are there already! Time flies!"
Bastard! He knew all the time.
He knows where we all reside.
"Be seeing you!" He whispered,
as he slid inside. "Have a nice day."

His last words hovered in the air.
"I shall have any sort of day I want."
I cried as I quickened my step.
Away! Away!

Am/Pm

In the morning,
the time of perfect quiet
when all the family
have not yet claimed our day,
I collapse so wonderfully.

How exact. How holy this silence.
The time of us, alone.
And not a sound of anything,
except Erica turning
the pages of The Times.
And me slowly stirring the soup;
and my heart stirring, stirring.
The smell permeating
this place. This precious space.

But soon the tribe!
Our beloveds, descending!
And later the feast of words;
all of us together. Loud, eating;
joking, laughing across the table.

Ellis! Ellis!

True friendship is a funny thing;
it digs deep. It's a bit like love.
Sometimes it caresses, sometimes it turns into tears.
Sometimes it cuts your guts to pieces.

How could you die?
Ellis! You have made us feel so mortal.
How could you do such a thing to us?
To yourself?

You, a doctor should have known better,
in this endless surgery called life.
How inconsiderate of you.
How could you dare to be so unreasonable?
Sometimes, when a friend dares to depart,
the pain tears your soul apart.
And the crowd left behind can do nothing.

This, Ellis is a lament, a fearsome love song
that stabs the heart.
It is three in the afternoon in this café
where time still exists.

But Ellis, you are gone;
sleeping without end
in the womb of nothingness.
Do not ask me to understand.
Every, every day
I understand less and less.

I sit here, in this café,
pulling these words out of my soul,
an endless ribbon of lament, threnody
and memory.

Ellis! Ellis! Off you went, impatient as ever,
leaving so many questions, shadows,
so may corners, where you still hover
above our talk, our sighs.
Our long dreams and shortening days,
as we endlessly recount moments.
Stories, quixotic flashes of the
paradox of this life.

Unique you were, and sometimes
ridiculous, my impossible friend,
and against all the odds,
a very, very human being.
Ellis! What an enigma you are.
So helpful, so concerned for others
and their needs.
Yet you turned a blind eye
to what was happening inside you.

Nobody like you will come this way again.
achieving all your backward somersaults;
imploding, exploding.
Irascible. Charming. Warm.
Constantly inconstant.
Contradicting yourself,
and the searching desire of all your days.

Ellis, it's over. All is forgiven, all is cancelled out.
You owe us nothing, but the warm laughter
that you evoke once the sorrow
and the weeping is past.

How can we ever forget
the unforgettable?
A friend so rare, tilting at all your windmills
on this breathless oasis called existence.

Ellis! You have gone into the great ocean.
A small boat, slipping away, lighting up
our dark for a small time.
But now that light has gone out
and you sail into the Great Goornicht.
Into that dark, that endless sea of nothingness.

Ellis! So soon. Too soon. Too sudden.
Without even a wave goodbye.
The wind moans deep through this
long night
and clouds race across the moon.
Lovers. Mothers, Fathers. Sisters.
Brothers. Aunts. Uncles. And yes! Friends! .
All pass away.

Ellis. Ellis.
Your name has become a sort of mantra.
Ellis! Ellis!
Alas.
Vale!

The Last Wave Goodbye
For Peggy

In the street small gatherings;
whispering bewilderment.
Astonishment! Have you heard the news?

Strange really, considering we all knew the score.
But you know, man,
Peggy was not like any other creature
in this crazy universe.

So Peggy has finally decided to not hang about;
to be around no longer.
Thus she finally departed this vale of fears
for somewhere far out in the firmament.
Somewhere far more permanent.

Listen! I can still hear her.

You see man, it's cool! Very, very cool!
And I've had enough and more than enough.
I'm off for that endless rave in the groovy grave.

Peggy could make a joke out of anything.
And death was just another joke.
And life.
Everything for Peggy was Send Up.

She was always more than enough.
You were either in or out.

Peggy was always in her skin,
but very, very way out.

So this is not the time for mourning.
But a time for jive and joint laughter,
so enjoy! Enjoy sweetheart!
Forget it man. Dance and sing and celebrate
while you can.

So, like I was saying. That glad mad bird
has finally flown; blown this cellar.
And all other humans who have come this way
have faded, have tended to blur and merge.

Peggy stood alone.
That genius of survival still lives in our laughter.
Pain was the main drag, man!
But every day she got through;
somehow.

Now the pain and Peggy have gone.
Listen! Now only her sighs linger;
echo.
Yet I see her even now,
watching, hiding in that mirror
called death.
She still loves company.

And there are many, many
squares hanging about, where she has gone.
She'll soon sort them out.

Peggy! Peggy! What else can I say?
You were so crazy, darling!
So miraculous and courageous.

And now you confront the ancient gods.
Poor sods!

Peggy! You will always live and be remembered
by the dust and bricks of these streets
you still inhabit.
Despite leaving the stage in the middle
of the scene.
Leaving us to sweep up and shrug and smile,
and even laugh as you walk away;
waving.

Old Happens

Old happens.
No need to go out of your way
to visit him.
Old comes to you.
No need to be concerned
about not hearing
the knock on the door.
Old needs no knock.
No door. No lock. No key.
He walks right through
the bricks of your life.
Old has the imperceptible trick
of entering your refuge
like a true friend you've known forever.
He sighs, smiles and whispers.
My dear friend
this is your end.

Only You Beneath The Moon And Under The Sun

In my sleep I wander the wastelands
of nowhere,
looking for a way in or out.

I dive upward to find her,
to close down my worlds of doubt.
My fear slopes away
when the sunlight hits the room.
And there she is, beside me
breathing in another day.
My wife.
Yes! I know this place.
This space. It is called life.

Anima

Once she gazed upon my face with adoration.
Now she brushes my mouth for crumbs.
Smoothes my shoulders, combs my hair,
so, so beautiful the way she hums.
She hands me a mirror, calls me handsome.
I see that time is not my friend.
She is my beginning, my middle
and my end.

Dramatist

Death with his hook
in the wings
looks my way.
He'll yank me offstage
by the end of the day.
He blows me a kiss,
I turn away.
He laughs and he laughs.
I get on with the play.

Lip Service

They congregate in synagogues
to pray
in a language they do not understand.
For their children they do not understand.

Song of the Hypochondriac

For Peter Majer, a fellow sufferer

Being human is dangerous
and possibly a waste of space.
The enemy within simply hides, waits,
bides his time.
So where shall I begin?
And where and when will I end?
My body is not my friend.

I have this pulsing pain
behind my eyes and through my heart,
which affects every part
of the angst in my pangst.
My pulsing blood at a stroke
floods my veins,
congeals the labyrinths of my pain.
Who I was shall never be again.

Every organ plays a threatening tocatta.
My inoperable maladies proliferate, inflate
my obscene shrieking spleen.
I await my inescapable fate.
My body, the bastard, my only enemy!

There is nowhere I can run.
I have swallowed, choked back
my pathetic pride.

Serenading my revolting innards,
my volcano of brain explodes,
sending fearsome songs to my wobbly feet.
It's getting dark. I am depleted, defeated
in my collapsing shattered world.
Oh, the bondage of my body!
My heartless heart.
Why me? Why me?
I am only eighty, and helpless.
And hopeless in this cage.
And slowly approaching
the foothills of middle age.

The Old Man

Nurse! Nurse!
Bring the bedpan
then wash me down
just one more time.

You shine amongst the stinking bodies.
You clear the dark that fogs the room.
Queen of Africa! Angel of mercy!
Oh, bring the bedpan! Please come quick.

Wash me down then lift me up.
Lift me high towards the sun.

Your Trousers

Your trousers are ready, Erica said
I've taken them up an inch or so.
You've shrunk a little,
but even so
your head it seems continues to grow.
Are you listening my love? Did you ever?
Were you ever prepared for inclement weather?
Your trousers are ready, Erica said

So I took them off and got into bed.

The Myrtle Bush

The myrtle bush
sings in the garden
under a black night.

When I open the door
she embraces me.
I close my eyes
and pull two leaves
from her branches,
and rub them between my fingers.

The perfume of the far off desert
assails the cold night air.

Flute and tambour dance me
into the communal garden.
Anyone peeping from the high
moon windows
must think I'm mad,
as I turn, faster and faster,
round and round,
over the wet grass.

Michael Kustow and the Angel of Death

The *Malach Hamovis* embraced you,
then withdrew;
overwhelmed perhaps
by your dazzling complexity.
She smiled,
waved goodbye and flew upward,
knowing she would have drowned
in the tears of those who love you.

So, you are too busy to die, my friend!
And you're at it again, five in the morning.
Having escaped the scythe,
you hear the piercing bugle call,
yet not to join the endless legions
who pass from light to endless night.

Instead you summon yourself
to the world of words, so on you go.
On and on. You have no choice.
Breathe deeply, oh my friend.
You are not and never were the dying sort.
And now dance to the trumpets
upon this parapet.

Rachel. Granddaughter

Death is before and after this life.
Yet life delivers us from the dead.

Out of the loins of Julie
comes Rachel.
This miracle from inner space,
hot from the cold universe.
And soon her hair of golden red
lights up our world.

To a Great Granddaughter

Rhianna has taken me hostage.
The manacles of her laughter
hold me in thrall.
On no account pay the ransom
or try to free me in anyway.

Anne Frank's Fragments from Nowhere

Sometimes, looking back I enter the
blue dream.
And again there is that place
called Earth! How beautiful.
How miraculously beautiful!

But all this is before . . . before . . .

I am thankful
I cannot penetrate the night and the fog
of the recent past.
But I can go further back.

Around a table, a family.
Laughter! They move,
proving again they are alive.
Yes! That is me! Over there,
standing on my chair.

My place, It was called home.
The only oasis.
A celebration in the endlessness of time.

Fragments! Time freezes. Snapshots.
My parents are getting married,
so now they are making love,
making me out of their laughter.

The moon scythes the night,
and stars my diadem,
cascade.
Dreams! Fragments from nowhere!

I see myself being born.
My mother and my father
delivering me on the white tablecloth;
between the candles and the plaited
Chola! Sabbath bread.

Moments flash. Fished out of the dark river.
Look! Me! Dancing!
All chronology, all laughter is lost.
Other scenes creep in.
Apparitions I cannot understand.
The house goes mad, talks to herself.
Pictures flying around the walls
are sucked out of windows no longer there.
Children are dying of old age.
The old eating their own flesh,
wander out in the middle of night
into locked playgrounds.

Snapshots. Bodies bent double
with joy.
They rush to swings, kicking the moon
with their toes. Sucking milk from each other.
Ravenous! Gurgling! Giggling!

Faces! Facets! Flashes!

Mother lights the candles,
her hands moving slowly through prayer,
and smoke.
Conjuring up golden flames;
lighting up the world.
Pushing skeins of warmth
towards me.
But again the dark descends.
The huddled ghosts wailing in chorus
must be heard again. And again.

Inmates dancing to the xylophone of bones.
Screaming so high in their skulls.
Sighs curl out of the Sea of Tears.
A whirlpool, sucking upwards
into God's gluttonous mouth.
The bastard!
He smiles, quenched with blood.
See! He slopes off again.

I do not understand this picture.
This fragment.
But I am there once more,
cupping my own ashes;
scattering myself on the moaning wind.

Yes! I remind myself,
once there was a place called earth.
We had a garden there.
My father died of life.
My mother died of death.

And my sister died over and over again.

But for me, the witness, somewhere beyond
this tangled wall of wire,
I live on with these dreams.
Again and again.
Dreams of somewhere else.
beyond the nightmare.

Now Contralto Typhus sings a lullaby.
We get on with our deaths.

Yet one word haunts.
Love!
I heard it once. I saw it being born;
before it flew away.
Maybe it will all come back to me.
The meaning.
This endless sea of snapshots. Waves.
Fragments. A blink of years.

Other spectres come to dance.
A grain of sand in the desert
of the everlasting.
The slopes of nothingness.
This insignificant speck of time
on the quilt of eternity.

I cannot look back, so I force my mind
forward,
to read the faces of the distant future.

To where I know laughter was.
And dancing. I float in and out
above the cymbals of chaos.

And look! I float.
Again I am holding out my hands
to greet you in my nothingness;
to dance with me.

This might then be called the song of hope.
The miraculous destiny of the tribe. Somehow.
Because I will always return
again and again. Against all the odds.
Evil and banality will one day be exorcised.
We cannot be erased. You'll see.
Hope transcends everything.
It comes when the flesh returns to the calling
bones.
When we fly out of earth and dust reassembles
skeleton.
The pull of time sucks me back into the dark.

Faces! Dreams! Lovers! Human dreams
are falling into the arms of space.
One moment more! One last fragment. Wait!
Hear me!
We fall in love and then and then –
Look! Hear me!
I dance. I dance to roll back fear and anger.

My song, my dance must cancel out
the prison ages of despair,
and only love exists.

Before there was . . . there was . . .
Anne! Forget. Forgive yourself.
Look forward. Hold on to the dream
and only see the worlds ahead.

Life is the beautiful light
in the entire darkness of time.
Look! I dance. Dance because
I believe that I existed
and I fell into love and I will exist
and love forever. Against all the odds.
Again and again.

We are beautiful. And yes, we are loving.
And we will love one another.
One day. All of us! Everywhere!
You'll see. Because there must be hope.

Before I go down into the dark,
into the night and fog, remember me.
And peace will come.
And a thousand centuries of leaves
and wind and rain and snows
will cover the snow; again and again.
And the snows will cover the snows
again and again.

Let me drink from the fountain of love.
I sing of the long tomorrow
when centuries and aeons will come and go
and people will come and go,
and fall in love. And be born and die.
And their children will be born
and smile and dance
and fall in love, and fall in love. Again and again.
And laugh. And dance.
These fragments. These moments
I hurl into the dark everlasting sky.
Confetti of dreams.

And peace will come.
And the tired will lie down and sleep.
And the dreamers will awake
and embrace the beauty
of world, of existence, of love.
And peace will come,
and love and lovers will transcend
the wars of earth.
And they will plant their love.
And the tree of love will grow forever.
And you'll see. Peace will come. And peace will come.
And people will come and go and live.
And live, again and again.
And peace will come. You'll see!
You'll see. And peace will come!
And peace will come!
And peace must come.

Dancing Partner

Our fifty years have just sailed by;
we laugh and wave them come and go.
So lean on me and give me strength
and I'll forgive you all my sins.

This Room in the Sunlight

This room in the sunlight.
And music weaving,
imploring from the other room.

And Erica! Her silhouette perched
over the newspaper;
sighing for the woes of the world.
Then she turns, her sadness, her smiles
coalesce, dance together
in those deep dark eyes.

This room in the morning.
And birds, the other side of glass,
darting through bare branches.
And the music slowly, slowing;
sewing sweet threnody.

This room in the sunlight.
Work soon! Not now,
soon, after coffee.
And my fingertips restless,
waiting.

But the web of sunlight
enclosing, disabling the turmoil,
the turbine of my brain.

This room in the morning.
And my heart full of loving;
and the calling laughter
of children not here.
And their lingering, echoing.

And Erica there, haloed by sunlight,
pouring gold into this space called
home; into this room in the sunlight
and the joy of living.